From Rapture to Eternity:

God's Plan For The Future

Disclaimer

Copyright © 2016 – All Rights Reserved

All rights reserved. No part of this publication may be reproduced, stored in a retrieval system, or transmitted by any means, without the prior permission in writing from the publisher, nor be otherwise circulated in any form of binding or cover other than that in which it is published and with a similar condition including this condition being imposed on the subsequent.

Dedication

My passion for Eschatology began with a Bible Doctrine class that I took in my first year in Bible College. I was intrigued that Christians could know so much about God's plan for the future. As I made my way through that course and my theology course on the same subject, I knew I was going to stay intrigued for a lifetime.

My theology professor, the late Dr. Hoyle Bowman, impressed upon me the need for proper biblical interpretation. His instructions have helped me develop this project. Therefore, I dedicate this book to his memory.

See you in the Big E real soon, Dr. B!

Preface

When it comes to prophecy in the Old and New Testament, we get a clue from the first few chapters of the Book of Revelation. When Jesus wrote letters to seven different churches, amazingly and coincidentally, those letters seemed to parallel church history. They follow church history all the way to the last letter, that John penned down from the Words of Jesus to the Laodicean church.

To those who have studied prophecy or who enjoy reading the Book of Revelation, it seems that we are living in the last days – the Laodicean days. We see a lot of information in the Scripture that points to the signs of the end of the church age. In the Last Days, men will be lovers of themselves – petty, high-minded, wicked, not for self, and not for god. Moreover, as it was in the days of Noah where everybody was doing what they wanted to do, so it would be in the End of Times.

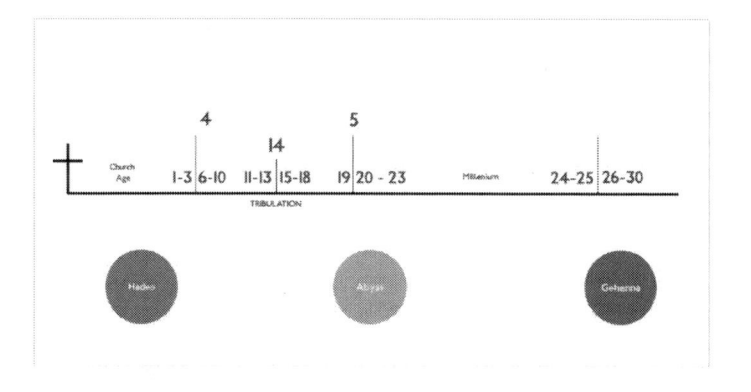

We'll visit Revelation a lot. I want to give you a broad perspective on what God wants to do and will be doing in the very near future, probably in our lifetime. Since we are near the end of the Church Age, we will be looking at a chart that helps us see the big picture.

Now to the right of the cross we have the church age that one day will be finished. Soon, Christ will come to get the Church. Once that happens, a specific time will begin on the Earth known as the Tribulation. It can be divided into two segments, Tribulation and the Great Tribulation. Then after the tribulation is finished, Christ comes back to Earth to set up the Millennium. The Millennium will be a period of thousand years where Christ will rule the Earth. After that, God will get rid of the Earth and all of Heaven and recreate it. Then Eternity reigns from there on out.

That is the broad picture. We will be covering 30 specific events that God has in store in the future, as is seen throughout the Scripture. Now, you can see that I have drawn three circles below the timeline. The first circle represents Hades or the Grave as it is called in the Old Testament. It is hell and the spirit of everyone who dies without Christ will be imprisoned there. One day, that is going to change because the hell as we see today will turn into Gehenna or Lake of Fire. The only difference between the two is that one day, Hades will give up all the souls in it to be judged and burned in the Lake of Fire. The torment will last forever and ever. The circle in the middle is the Bottomless Pit or the Abyss. It is a holding place. The third circle is Gehenna or the Lake of Fire.

In order to get the perspective that I am about to share here, you need to be familiar with a few basic concepts that are a part of Scripture. First of all, I think one of the biggest mistakes that teachers and preachers make is that they don't separate Israel from the church. They kind of lump them together. That is not the case in the Bible. We have the Old Covenant and the New Covenant. The old one is centered on Israel and all that God did throughout the Old Testament since the beginning of time. Then the New Testament begins with Christ in the gospels. Then at Pentecost, the Church Age began. Forty days after the Resurrection, the Holy Spirit came and the Church was birthed. By keeping Israel and the Church separate, it will be easier to understand how God is going to unfold these 30 events in a natural and organized fashion.

Secondly, in my approach to prophecy, I emphasize two major events. First is the pre tribulation rapture of Church. That's a very big event. Christ comes to get the Church before Rapture begins. Some experts believe that Christ comes in the middle of the Tribulation to get the Church so that it escapes the Great tribulation. However, my position is different. In all the information that we find on the tribulation, none of it applies to the Church and all of it applies to Israel. After chapter 4, you see no mention of the Church in the Book of Revelation for a good reason. The Church is not mentioned. The tribulation is not meant for the Church but for the Jews – the time of Jacob's trouble. Throughout both Testaments, the tribulation is directly tied to the Jews.

Contents

From Rapture to Eternity:
God's Plan For The Future

Disclaimer

Dedication

Preface

Introduction

Event # 1: Rapture

Event # 2: Resurrection of Dead Saints

Event # 3: Translation of Living Saints

Event # 4: Judgment of Rewards for Christians

Event #5: Marriage Supper of the Lamb

Event # 6: The Revived Roman Empire

Event #7: The Rise of the Antichrist

Recap of first seven events

Event #8: Signing of the peace Treaty

Event #9 144,002 Witnesses Ministering Publicly

Event # 10: Northern Coalition Attacking Israel

event # 11: antichrist wounded, recovers, worshipped

Event # 12: The False Prophet

event #13 one-world government, economy, religion develops

Event # 14: The Antichrist Breaks the Peace Treaty with Israel

Event # 15: The Saints Are Persecuted

Event # 16: Apostate World-Church Gets Destroyed

Event # 17: Cataclysmic Judgments of God

Event # 18: Collapse of the World Commercial System

Event # 19: Armageddon

Event # 20: Appearance of Christ on Earth

Event # 21: Binding of Satan In the Bottomless Pit

EVENT #22 Millennium

Event # 23: Resurrection of Tribulation Saints

Event # 24: Satan Freed From The Bottomless Pit

Event # 25: Satan Leads Unsaved Men Against God

Event # 26: Satan Defeated

Event # 27: Satan Cast Into The Lake Of Fire

Event # 28: Great White Throne of Judgment & Resurrection of Unsaved Dead

Event # 29: Judgment of Sin & Punishment of Lake of Fire

Event # 30: New Heaven, Earth, And Jerusalem

Conclusion

Introduction

I have a passion for prophecy. I began studying prophecy over three decades ago. Since then, I have been trying to understand God's plan for the future. God has a lot to say about that in Scripture. He sees everything from the beginning to the end. My desire has been to get a broad picture of that plan and share it with everybody who wants to hear it.

Eschatology is the doctrine of last things. Prophecy has a twofold meaning. There are two types of prophecies: 1) predicting what was about to happen 2) relay a message from God. Either foretold or forth told; either type, the source of the message was from God.

I am a prophet myself in the sense that I forth tell what the Holy Spirit shows me. I don't predict what is going to happen. Instead, I just relay the message that we already have in a complete form i.e. prophecy. The Bible contains everything we need to know about the future. I want to share that with you in a way that's understandable. Thus, I will be *forth telling* what God has *foretold*. I hope that when we're through, you'll be able to understand what God has in store for all of us.

Before we get to the future, we need to get a picture of where we are at present. The first few chapters of the book of Revelation give us a good clue as to where we are on God's prophetic calendar. Many scholars today believe that we are living in the Laodicean Age. In the seventh letter to the church at Laodicea, Jesus described the people of Laodicea as being neither hot nor cold but lukewarm towards keeping God's faith. Complacency seems to be the theme of the day in our churches around the world too. The average church member is neither cold towards the Lord nor totally dedicated.

I believe we are living in the last days of the Church Age. I will be using a time chart in this book. It consists of three basic parts: the first of which is the Church Age. The second part is the Tribulation while the Millennium & recreation forms the third part. In our study of 30 events, I will be referring to this timeline frequently.

However, first, I would like to set the stage. Scripture has a lot to say about the signs of the time during the last days. Many of these signs can be seen happening today. I think the biggest sign took place 69 years ago when in 1948 Israel became a nation once again. Many Jews are returning to the land after some 2,000 years of being spread all over the world.

Paul described to Timothy what it would be like in the last days. Men will be lovers of themselves, lovers of money, boasters, proud, blasphemers, disobedient to parents, unthankful, unholy, unloving, unforgiving, slanderers, without self-control, brutal, despisers of good, traitors, headstrong, haughty, lovers of pleasure, rather than lovers of God, having a form of godliness but denying its power.

Event # 1: Rapture

Let us begin with the next great prophetic event that will probably happen in our 'lifetime or the Rapture. You won't find the word in the bible. The word is a Latin term, *raptore*, or caught up. We need to make sure that when this happens, if we are not already in heaven, 'that we go up with all other believers'.

This book was written to the believers of the church at Thessalonica who were struggling with the issue about what happens to those who have accepted Christ and have already died. They were concerned they had missed this event that Paul had mentioned in the last part of this chapter.

1 Thessalonians 4:13-17

I don't want you to be ignorant concerning those who have fallen asleep lest you sorrow as others who have no hope. For we believe that Jesus died and rose again, even so God would bring with him those who sleep in Jesus. For this, we say to you by the word of the Lord, that we who are alive and remain until the coming of the Lord will by no means precede those died who are asleep. For the Lord himself will descend from heaven, with a shout with the voice of an archangel and with a trumpet of God and the dead in Christ will rise first. And we are alive and remain, shall be caught up together with them in the clouds to meet the Lord in the air. And thus, we shall always be with the Lord. Therefore, comfort one another with these words.

This passage relates to us as believers, regardless of what church we belong to. Anyone who accepts Christ as their Savior is automatically placed in the Universal Church made up of believers from all over the world. Most of the time the word Church in the New Testament, refers to the local church. In particular, Paul was referring to the Church that the Lord had helped him establish in Thessalonica. They were wondering if they were going to be left behind and what will happen to their loved ones who had already died. When any believer in Christ takes their last breath, their body remains but their spirit immediately goes up to the Lord and remains there until this event.

Event # 2: Resurrection of Dead Saints

1 Corinthians 15:51-58

Behold, I tell you a mystery: We shall not all sleep, but we shall all be changed—In a moment, in the twinkling of an eye, at the last trumpet. For the trumpet will sound, and the dead will be raised incorruptible, and we shall be changed. 53 For this corruptible must put on incorruption, and this mortal must put on immortality. 54 So when this corruptible has put on incorruption, and this mortal has put on immortality, then shall be brought to pass the saying that is written: "Death is swallowed up in victory."55 "O Death, where is your sting?O Hades, where is your victory?"56 The sting of death is sin, and the strength of sin is the law. 57 But thanks be to God, who gives us the victory through our Lord Jesus Christ.58 Therefore, my beloved brethren, be steadfast, immovable, always abounding in the work of the Lord, knowing that your labor is not in vain in the Lord.

When the Rapture takes place, it is going to be fast. Blink your eye and it would be over. The Rapture will be over in 1/100th of a second! Picture every Christian gone in the blink of an eye, leaving behind a catastrophe. However, thank God, those who believe won't have to be concerned about what happens afterwards.

The souls of all believers in heaven will be reunited with what will be left of their bodies here on earth. At this union, they will receive their glorified bodies similar to the one Christ has.

Event # 3: Translation of Living Saints

Look at the passage in 1 Thessalonians again; it mentions that the Dead in Christ will start ascending before us. The third part of the Rapture is known as the Translation of the Living Saints. Those who are still alive, according to both passages, will bypass death. In other words, they won't have to die. They will be automatically changed. Picture how you are now. Then in the blink of an eye, you become mentally, physically, and spiritually perfect.

I like this because when we get changed, we get a body like Christ got at the first Easter. Why is this fantastic? For various reasons: After resurrection, did Christ eat? Yes, he did! On numerous occasions, he ate while in his resurrected body. I like that because I like to eat. So, it is good to know that we can eat throughout eternity. I will be able to eat as much as I want without any side effects.

That is only one benefit. Another thing that I like to do is to travel. Now, when we get a body like Jesus, there won't be any need for transportation. This event is actually a transportation event. When it happens, we will be off of this planet and in Heaven. When one soul leaves this world and goes to the next, regardless of which direction, it happens quickly.

I have read about a number of experiences of those who were on their way but came back. Perhaps this happened because God's time for their departure wasn't right. Could that be? God's timing is perfect. In fact, only God knows our time of departure. I find it intriguing that even Jesus doesn't know when the Rapture will take place; only the Father knows. It's good to know that before the Rapture takes place we can be assured that we will be with God. So, if we get this event right, we will be at peace for eternity.

Events 1-3 deal with the Rapture. When the Church has been

removed from this Earth, it will be in heaven. As soon as this happens, the next event i.e. Tribulation will unfold on Earth. This begs us to consider the question:

How can we be sure that the Rapture will be a Pre-Tribulation event?

The term, church, is used almost 20 times in Revelations 1-3 and then once at the end i.e. 22: 16. Revelations 1-3 seem to parallel church history. However, after chapter 3, there is no mention of the term, church, throughout the Tribulation period. There is only mention of the tribulation saints (those who refuse the mark of the beast and accept the message of salvation).

Dr. Tim La Haye lists four other reasons why the Rapture will precede the tribulation:

1. The Lord Himself promised to deliver us
2. Only this view preserves imminency
3. The church is to be delivered from the wrath (tribulation) to come (1 Thessalonians 1:10).
4. Christians are not appointed to wrath (1 Thessalonians. 5:9)

While events 6-18 would take place on earth the next two (4 and 5) events would take place in heaven.

---

[1]"Understanding Bible Prophecy for Yourself" pg. 79-82

Event # 4: Judgment of Rewards for Christians

Only two church events take place in heaven for the entire 7 years. The first event is known as the Judgment of Rewards for Christians.

This will be the first of two major judgments in Prophecy. One judgment would be for those who believe: the Old Testament and New Testament Saints. The other will be the Great White Throne judgment (which I will cover at the end of the book. It will be for all the unbelievers. This first one is also called the Judgment Seat of Christ. I also call it the Bema Seat. The best way to imagine what it would look like is the raised platform that marching bands stop in front of. On the platform would be sitting judges who will rate the performances. Only, it won't be the marching bands whose performance will be judged but ours.

2 Corinthians 5:9-11
Therefore we make it our aim, whether present or absent, to be well pleasing to Him. 10 For we must all appear before the judgment seat of Christ, that each one may receive the things done in the body, according to what he has done, whether good or bad. 11 Knowing, therefore, the terror of the Lord, we persuade men; but we are well known to God, and I also trust are well known in your consciences.

The Judgment Seat of Christ is reward-based. Every Christian will stand in front of Christ and be judged on the quality of their Christian service from the time that they became Christians to the time they died. Each believer will not be judged for sin since Christ took care of that at Calvary. "Good" and "Bad" 'refers to quality of ministry. The motive will be at the heart of the results. Self-centered ministry represents bad. Selfless ministry represents good.

1 CORINTHIANS 3:12-15

Now if anyone builds on this foundation with gold, silver, precious stones, wood, hay, straw, 13 each one's work will become clear; for the Day will declare it, because it will be revealed by fire; and the fire will test each one's work, of what sort it is. 14 If anyone's work which he has built on it endures, he will receive a reward. 15 If anyone's work is burned, he will suffer loss; but he himself will be saved, yet so as through fire.

Look at the materials listed in the passage above, i.e. gold, silver, precious stones, wood, hay, and straw. Fire is what tests the works. What are the works? I believe there will be a revealing of opportunities missed in serving the Lord. For the opportunities that we did not miss, our motives will be tested. If we did it for the wrong reasons, then the Fire is going to test it and it will be burned up, just as fire destroys wood, hay, and straw.

Paul mentioned that he dreaded this day. If he dreaded this day, then we need to take it serious too. If every Old and New Testament believer is to be judged one at a time, the process is going to be an extensive one. I believe it will take most of the seven years to be completed.

After each believer has been judged by fire, what is left would actually belong to the Lord because it is the Spirit that does the work; the believer only cooperates. Whatever good we do is what the Lord uses us to do. So, since He does the work, we should want to give all those rewards back to Him.

Speaking of rewards, there will be crowns that we can receive after judgment.

Among the rewards that can be earned are five types of crowns. These include:

1. Rejoicing (1 Thessalonians 2:19)
2. Incorruptible (1 Corinthians 9:25)
3. Glory (1 Peter 5:4)
4. Righteousness (2 Timothy 4:8)
5. Life (Revelation 2:10)

Crown of Rejoicing

This crown will be the reward of the soul winner.

1 Thessalonians 2:19-20

For what is our hope, or joy, or crown of rejoicing? Is it not even you in the presence of our Lord Jesus Christ at His coming? 20 For you are our glory and joy.

Philippians 4:1

Therefore, my beloved and longed-for brethren, my joy and crown, so stand fast in the Lord, beloved.

God desires to evangelize the lost and He promises rewards that will last eternally for those who seek such people out. The seeking out should be taken as a team effort of believers, so that both who sow and reap can enjoy the benefits together.

Incorruptible Crown

This crown will be presented to those who do not allow the world to squeeze them into it's mould. Their practical sanctification will stem from their devotion to God in order to be fit for ministry.

1 Corinthians 9:25

And everyone who competes for the prize is temperate in all things.

Now they do it to obtain a perishable crown, but we for an imperishable crown.

Crown of Glory

Peter 5:2-4

Shepherd the flock of God which is among you, serving as overseers, not by compulsion but willingly, not for dishonest gain but eagerly; nor as being lords over those entrusted to you, but being examples to the flock; and when the Chief Shepherd appears, you will receive the crown of glory that does not fade away.

This crown is for those who dedicate their lives to teaching the Word of God. It includes, but is not limited to pastors.

Crown of Righteousness

This crown is reserved for believers who have waited for their Lord's return anxiously. Such people would spend their lives in obedience of the Lord's commands. The crown is a reward for the believers who kept the faith that they need to await the return alive.

2 Timothy 4:6-8

For I am already being poured out as a drink offering, and the time of my departure is at hand. 7 I have fought the good fight, I have finished the race, I have kept the faith. 8 Finally, there is laid up for me the crown of righteousness, which the Lord, the righteous Judge, will give to me on that Day, and not to me only but also to all who have loved His appearing.

Crown of Life

Revelation 2:10

Do not fear any of those things which you are about to suffer. Indeed, the devil is about to throw some of you into prison, that you may be tested, and you will have tribulation ten days. Be faithful until death, and I will give you the crown of life.

This crown will be the reward for people who remained faithful when circumstances became adverse. They received the trials that the Lord set before them with joy and considered them as opportunities to grow. They overcame these trials by letting their love for the Lord motivate them to see it through. When Israel was beset with wilderness trials, they failed to do so and forgot that God was on their side.

These rewards fit the category of gold, silver, and precious stones which fire does not destroy.

Event #5: Marriage Supper of the Lamb

While we are being judged in Heaven, many things will be happening down on Earth. This second event in Heaven will take place near the end of the Tribulation. Therefore, after we have been judged, received new clothing, and are all cleaned up it will be time to celebrate. In your mind, go back to the upper room, that night when Jesus was with the disciples instituting the New Covenant. He said, "I will not drink of this wine again until I enter into the Kingdom". That means Jesus will not drink wine until this event preceding the Millennium.

Revelation 19:7
Let us be glad and rejoice and give Him glory, for the marriage of the Lamb has come, and His wife has made herself ready. 8 And to her it was granted to be arrayed in fine linen, clean and bright, for the fine linen is the righteous acts of the saints.

Revelation 19:9
Then he said to me, "Write: 'Blessed are those who are called to the marriage supper of the Lamb!'" And he said to me, "These are the true sayings of God."

The Marriage Supper is going to be a beautiful event for all the Saints. You and I are Saints because of what Christ did. The concept of the marriage supper in the culture of that day was that this supper was held at the end of the marriage ceremony. Everybody got together to share a meal which could go on for days, even weeks. It is supposed to be a glorious time where no one is in a hurry.

Some scholars differ as to where this event will happen. I don't think it will happen on Earth. I believe it will take place in heaven at the end of the Tribulation, preceding the Second Coming Of

Christ. So during the Tribulation the Judgment of Rewards and the Marriage of the Lamb will take place in heaven.

Since the Rapture removes the church, imagine the chaos that will ensue. Picture a Christian airline pilot and co-pilot at the helm of the plane when the Rapture will take place. It would be a disaster! Following the Rapture, the whole earth will be affected. This includes the Jews since they didn't accept Christ as their Savior at his first coming. This seven-year period also known as the 70th Week of Daniel was designed to get them ready for His second Coming.

I cover fourteen events will take place on Earth during the seven years while we the church will be in heaven. When the restraining influence of the Holy Spirit leaves this world at the Rapture, Satan will have his way with this world, but only for a short time.

Let's turn our attention to the next 14 events on earth during the Tribulation.

Event # 6: The Revived Roman Empire

Two places that mention this event include the Books of Daniel and Revelation. The Revived Roman Empire in Daniel's vision was part of a huge statue. The statue has feet made of iron mixed with clay. That symbolizes the revival of the Roman Empire. It is going to be powered by Satan himself. John recorded a vision that builds upon Daniel's vision of a statue, representing world kingdoms, particularly of the feet of iron mixed with clay.

Revelation 13:1
Then I stood on the sand of the sea. And I saw a beast rising up out of the sea, having seven heads and ten horns, and on his horns ten crowns, and on his heads a blasphemous name.

This revived empire is going to be a confederacy of ten European nations through which the Antichrist will seize control. I believe, this empire is already in its initial form i.e. the European Union. Don't get hung up on the number of countries involved. Keep in mind that it will develop into the greatest power on Earth. This empire is going to strengthen itself and take over the whole world.

As a sideline note, I want to point out that nowhere in Scripture will you find the name of our country. It is not in the Bible. I don't know what that means. I can only go by what I find in Scripture. When we talk about this sixth event, the United States is not mentioned. Obviously, we have only been around for a couple of hundred years. God has blessed us because we sought Him out in the beginning. Just because we are not mentioned, we can't conclude we will no longer be around come tribulation time.

However, in our day, the European Union made developments that seem to fall in line with what Daniel saw in his vision about the revived Roman Empire. Think of the political system that is mentioned in Revelation as an evolved form of the common economy system, such as the EU.

Before BREXIT, a Canadian documentary on the EU, *Birth of a Superstate*, mentioned that Western Europe (WE) would soon replace the world's current political centre. Thus, as foretold, there could easily be a common currency, one central bank, and the political potential required for WE to take over the world.

The territory of the Old Roman Empire is as big as the Europe of today. Therefore, after the Rapture, it will revive and quickly move to dominate the whole world similar in power to the original one.

In this ten-nation confederacy, one individual will become prominent and rule it. This brings us to the next event.

Event #7: The Rise of the Antichrist

Revelation 13:2

Now the beast which I saw was like a leopard, his feet were like the feet of a bear, and his mouth like the mouth of a lion. The dragon gave him his power, his throne, and great authority. 3 And I saw one of his heads as if it had been mortally wounded, and his deadly wound was healed. And all the world marveled and followed the beast. 4 So they worshiped the dragon who gave authority to the beast; and they worshiped the beast, saying, "Who is like the beast? Who is able to make war with him?"

5 And he was given a mouth speaking great things and blasphemies, and he was given authority to continue for forty-two months. 6 Then he opened his mouth in blasphemy against God, to blaspheme His name, His tabernacle, and those who dwell in heaven. 7 It was granted to him to make war with the saints and to overcome them. And authority was given him over every tribe, tongue, and nation. 8 All who dwell on the earth will worship him, whose names have not been written in the Book of Life of the Lamb slain from the foundation of the world.

9 If anyone has an ear, let him hear.

Who are the ones included in the Trinity today? The Bible lists the Father, Son, and the Holy Spirit in the Trinity.

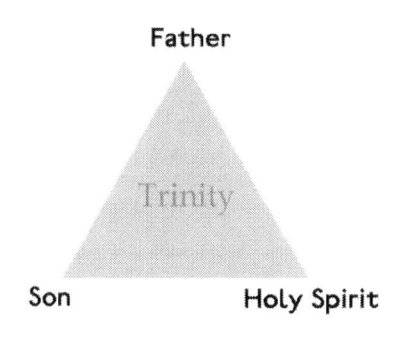

When true spiritual guidance is removed from this Earth, Satan will form an evil trinity. To imitate the Father, we have the Dragon, which is Satan himself. It comes as no surprise since Satan still wants to be greater than his Creator. The second part of this evil trinity is the Antichrist, the fake Jesus. The whole world, including Israel, will buy into it, thinking he is the real Messiah. Then to imitate the Holy Spirit is the False Prophet. The False Prophet will arrive on the scene and unite the whole world into one church, and then try to get it to worship the Antichrist. During the seven-year period, the fake trinity will develop, then fall apart.

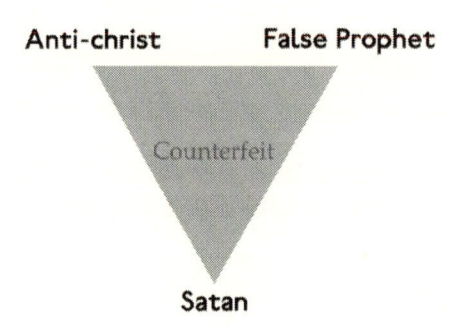

```
        Anti-christ      False Prophet

                  Counterfeit

                    Satan
```

DANIEL 7:8

I was considering the horns, and there was another horn, a little one, coming up among them, before whom three of the first horns were plucked out by the roots. And there, in this horn, were eyes like the eyes of a man, and a mouth speaking pompous words.

DANIEL 7:19-25

Then I wished to know the truth about the fourth beast, which was different from all the others, exceedingly dreadful, with its teeth of iron and its nails of bronze, which devoured, broke in pieces, and trampled the residue with its feet; 20 and the ten horns that were on its head, and the other horn which came up, before which three fell, namely, that horn which had eyes and a mouth which spoke pompous words, whose appearance was greater than his fellows.

21 "I was watching; and the same horn was making war against the saints, and prevailing against them, 22 until the Ancient of Days came, and a judgment was made in favor of the saints of the Most High, and the time came for the saints to possess the kingdom. 23 "Thus he said: 'The fourth beast shall be A fourth kingdom on earth, Which shall be different from all other kingdoms, And shall devour the whole earth, Trample it and break it in pieces. 24 The ten horns are ten kings Who shall arise from this kingdom. And another shall rise after them; He shall be different from the first ones, And shall subdue three kings. 25 He shall speak pompous words against the Most High, Shall persecute the saints of the Most High, And shall intend to change times and law. Then the saints shall be given into his hand For a time and times and half a time.

Let us simplify the information mentioned above. This confederacy will have an eleventh king (little horn) rising to the surface, the Antichrist. Three kings will not cooperate with him and the Antichrist will get rid of these dissident kings. Then he will take control of the confederacy. This would make his rule transform from ruling a localized territory to commanding something as extensive as the Old Roman Empire. Next, he will quickly conquer the entire world. Thus, this will form a one-world economy, one-world church, and one-world government during the early stages of the Tribulation. However, this will happen only to fall apart when Christ comes back and changes everything. People will think that the Millennium has already begun because the Antichrist will be able to solve the world's major problems. The Antichrist will be an intelligent super human being empowered by Satan and setting out to conquer the world.

If the rapture took place today and you were left behind, it will mean in your head, you had the knowledge about Jesus but didn't accept Christ as your Savior with your heart.

There can be only one Antichrist and all the others like him are considered as prototypes. Listed below are characteristics of the Antichrist:

1. He will come into power when the world is about to end:

DANIEL 8:23

"And in the latter time of their kingdom, When the transgressors have reached their fullness, A king shall arise, Having fierce features, Who understands sinister schemes.

2. His power will extend to the farthest reaches of the world:

REVELATION 13:7

It was granted to him to make war with the saints and to overcome them. And authority was given him over every tribe, [a] tongue, and nation.

3. He will rule the world from Rome:

REVELATION 13:8-9

All who dwell on the earth will worship him, whose names have not been written in the Book of Life of the Lamb slain from the foundation of the world. 9 If anyone has an ear, let him hear.

4. He would be smart and charming:

DANIEL 7:20

and the ten horns that were on its head, and the other horn which came up, before which three fell, namely, that horn which had eyes and a mouth which spoke pompous words, whose appearance was greater than his fellows.

5. He will have the whole world's consent to rule:

REVELATION 17:12-13

"The ten horns which you saw are ten kings who have received no kingdom as yet, but they receive authority for one hour as kings

with the beast. 13 These are of one mind, and they will give their power and authority to the beast.

6. He will allow deceit to prosper:

DANIEL 8:24-25
His power shall be mighty, but not by his own power;
He shall destroy fearfully,
And shall prosper and thrive;
He shall destroy the mighty, and also the holy people.
25 "Through his cunning
He shall cause deceit to prosper under his rule;
And he shall exalt himself in his heart.
He shall destroy many in their prosperity.
He shall even rise against the Prince of princes;
But he shall be broken without human means.

7. He will also be controlling global economy:

REVELATION 13:16-17
He causes all, both small and great, rich and poor, free and slave, to receive a mark on their right hand or on their foreheads, 17 and that no one may buy or sell except one who has the mark or the name of the beast, or the number of his name.

8. He will unite himself with Israel.

DANIEL 9:27
Then he shall confirm a covenant with many for one week;
But in the middle of the week
He shall bring an end to sacrifice and offering.
And on the wing of abominations shall be one who makes desolate,
Even until the consummation, which is determined,
Is poured out on the desolate.

9. He will then dissolve his treaty with Israel by attacking it.

Daniel 9:26

And the people of the prince who is to come
Shall destroy the city and the sanctuary.
The end of it shall be with a flood,
And till the end of the war desolations are determined.

10. He will deify himself:

2 Thessalonians 2:4

He will oppose and he will exalt himself over everything that is called God or is worshipped, so that he sets himself up in God's temple, proclaiming himself to be God.

There are other details about the Antichrist given in the Bible as well. However, there is no mention of whether he will be Jewish or not. He might also be a Gentile. It is evident, however, that he will form the last great Gentile kingdom and rule the world from his seat in the West. [2]

---

[2] Ed Hindson pg. 26, 27 The Popular Encyclopedia Of Bible Prophecy

Recap of first seven events

Once the Father tells Jesus to go get his children, the Church, there would be a loud trumpet blast. In a split second, the heavenly souls will be reunited with new bodies. This is the Rapture. Other believers who are still alive will bypass death, get their glorified bodies, and go to heaven, staying with Christ forever and ever.

Different events will be happening back on Earth. Of the 30 events that we will talk about, almost half of them will take place down here, during the 7-year period while the church is in heaven. Tribulation will occur, namely the 70th week of Daniel. Each week represents 7 years. Sixty-nine of those 7 year sets have already happened in history. The last and worst set of 7 years is imminent, any day now.

The purpose of the enemy would be to counterfeit the Millennium or the true reign of Christ. Satan always wants to deceive and gain control and be like God or even greater than Him. Now that the end of the Church Age is near, Satan knows his time is drawing to a close. Soon, God will cast Satan out of heaven, never to come back to accuse His believers. Once he is back on Earth, Satan will build a fake Millennium.

Event #8: Signing of the peace treaty

The tribulation doesn't really begin until this happens. The Antichrist will sign a 7-year agreement with Israel to allow them to worship as they 'see fit. They will also be promised protection.

Daniel 9:27

Then he shall confirm a covenant with many for one week;
But in the middle of the week
He shall bring an end to sacrifice and offering.
And on the wing of abominations shall be one who makes desolate,
Even until the consummation, which is determined,
Is poured out on the desolate.

So here, we see that a peace treaty is signed by the Antichrist who will rule this revived Roman Empire centered around Europe. He will promise to let them do their thing for 7 years. In order for the Levites to offer sacrifices what has to happen? A temple has to be built. Whether construction coincides with signing or shortly after, it must be built during the first half of the Tribulation.

Jerusalem has a central location called the Temple Mount. Today, the temple is not there. This mosque or the Dome of the Rock is considered a holy site for Muslims who trace their lineage back to Ishmael. It is sitting on Mount Moriah where Abraham sacrificed Isaac. Before the temple was built, God had them use a portable temple called the Tabernacle. Wherever God moved Israel, the tabernacle went as well. When David came to power, he wanted to build a permanent structure. He wasn't allowed to build it due to the prolific bloodshed from war. So, Solomon built the temple.

I have met the man whose passion is to build the next temple. On separate occasions, he even tried to take the cornerstone of the next temple and place it on the temple mount but was met with too much opposition. Gershon Salomon is his name. He and devout Levites are ready to build the temple today.

There is consideration for an alternate site on the temple mount. If that does happen, it may be in conjunction with leaving the Dome of Rock in its place. If the temple construction began today, I believe it would cause a holy war or jihad between Muslims, Jews, and other nations. I personally don't think construction begins until the Antichrist makes this covenant.

If temple construction does begin in our lifetime, we had better be listening for that trumpet blast. Sure up your salvation today. I believe we are very close. Don't get left behind. This peace treaty when signed will allow the Israelites to start temple worship again.

Event #9 144,002 Witnesses Ministering Publicly

When the Church is removed from Earth global chaos will ensue. The Holy Spirit has a restraining influence over sin in today's world, not so much during the Tribulation. If you get left behind, miss the Rapture, you could still accept Christ as Savior. The gospel will be proclaimed by Spirit filled and sealed Jewish evangelists (12,000 from each tribe).

REVELATION 7:4-8

And I heard the number of those who were sealed. One hundred and forty-four thousand of all the tribes of the children of Israel were sealed:
5 of the tribe of Judah twelve thousand were sealed;
of the tribe of Reuben twelve thousand were sealed;
of the tribe of Gad twelve thousand were sealed;
6 of the tribe of Asher twelve thousand were sealed;
of the tribe of Naphtali twelve thousand were sealed;
of the tribe of Manasseh twelve thousand were sealed;
7 of the tribe of Simeon twelve thousand were sealed;
of the tribe of Levi twelve thousand were sealed;
of the tribe of Issachar twelve thousand were sealed;
8 of the tribe of Zebulun twelve thousand were sealed;
of the tribe of Joseph twelve thousand were sealed;
of the tribe of Benjamin twelve thousand were sealed.

"They will embark on their ministry of preaching the gospel to those who have been left behind. These servants will experience incredible results. The text does not specifically call them witnesses but the proclamation of the gospel is one of their primary functions [3]

---

[3]." Tim LaHaye, 'the Popular Encyclopedia of Bible Prophecy' pg.

Accepting Christ as Savior will come with a heavy price tag. Many who refuse the mark of the beast will be eliminated. Why refuse it unless you accept the message of the 144,000? More on tribulation saints and mark of the beast later.

Let's consider the two witnesses.

REVELATION 11:3-10

And I will give power to my two witnesses, and they will prophesy one thousand two hundred and sixty days, clothed in sackcloth."

4 These are the two olive trees and the two lampstands standing before the God of the earth. 5 And if anyone wants to harm them, fire proceeds from their mouth and devours their enemies. And if anyone wants to harm them, he must be killed in this manner. 6 These have power to shut heaven, so that no rain falls in the days of their prophecy; and they have power over waters to turn them to blood, and to strike the earth with all plagues, as often as they desire.

7 When they finish their testimony, the beast that ascends out of the bottomless pit will make war against them, overcome them, and kill them. 8 And their dead bodies will lie in the street of the great city which spiritually is called Sodom and Egypt, where also our Lord was crucified. 9 Then those from the peoples, tribes, tongues, and nations will see their dead bodies three-and-a-half days, and not allow their dead bodies to be put into graves. 10 And those who dwell on the earth will rejoice over them, make merry, and send gifts to one another, because these two prophets tormented those who dwell on the earth.

I believe these two witnesses are literally Moses and Elijah coming back to Earth during the tribulation. What they do parallels what Moses and Elijah did their first time around. Closely connected is

---

256, 257

their appearance on the Mount of Transfiguration. Before Jesus took on his former glory atop the mountain, He brought with Him Peter, James, and John. Who else appeared? Moses and Elijah. I believe that they will also be the two witnesses for God during the first half of the Tribulation (verse 3). These two witnesses will be empowered by God to perform similar miracles unharmed due to His protection. But Satan will then be allowed to kill them, only for God to resurrect them three days later while the celebrating world will watch in horror.

So grace will be extended to the world during the Tribulation. Mankind will have opportunity to turn to Christ for salvation. Ultimately, all will make the choice for Him or take the mark of the beast and be doomed for Hell. Choosing Jesus will probably result in martyrdom, but there will be few who escape the Antichrist's grasp.

Event # 10: Northern Coalition Attacking Israel

This event would probably occur during the first half of the Tribulation. During the Tribulation, a build up will take place, which will include the building of one-world system, government, and economy. Then it will fall apart within this 7 yr. timeframe. The particular group of countries who will be a part of this one-world church will include Russia, Ukraine, Iran, Kazakhstan, Sudan, Libya, Turkey, and Saudi Arabia. This coalition will come together to attack Israel on their own accord, apparently challenging the Antichrist. They will decide so, to invade Israel for its wealth, and its land.

During their advance, God will intervene:

Ezekiel 38:18-22

"And it will come to pass at the same time, when Gog comes against the land of Israel," says the Lord God, "that My fury will show in My face. 19 For in My jealousy and in the fire of My wrath I have spoken: 'Surely in that day there shall be a great earthquake in the land of Israel, 20 so that the fish of the sea, the birds of the heavens, the beasts of the field, all creeping things that creep on the earth, and all men who are on the face of the earth shall shake at My presence. The mountains shall be thrown down, the steep places shall fall, and every wall shall fall to the ground.' 21 I will call for a sword against Gog throughout all My mountains," says the Lord God. "Every man's sword will be against his brother. 22 And I will bring him to judgment with pestilence and bloodshed; I will rain down on him, on his troops, and on the many peoples who are with him, flooding rain, great hailstones, fire, and brimstone.

Chapter 39 deals with the aftermath.

Before we get to our next event, let's recap the development of the Antichrist. The tribulation will officially begin with the 7-year peace treaty. Within the first 3 ½ years, Israel will peacefully dwell in the land with temple worship firmly in place. All will seem well under the Antichrist who will then lead his confederation toward a counterfeit millennium (event 13). The only fly in the ointment seems to be event 10. This leads us to one of our most pivotal passages in the first half of the Tribulation.

REVELATION 13: 1-2

Then I stood on the sand of the sea. And I saw a beast rising up out of the sea, having seven heads and ten horns, and on his horns ten crowns, and on his heads a blasphemous name. 2 Now the beast which I saw was like a leopard, his feet were like the feet of a bear, and his mouth like the mouth of a lion. The dragon gave him his power, his throne, and great authority.

Here, the beast is the confederacy described as a combination of Daniel's vision of former worldwide kingdoms (leopard, bear, lion). The dragon is Satan himself. Now:

EVENT # 11: ANTICHRIST WOUNDED, RECOVERS, WORSHIPPED

REVELATION 13:3-5
And I saw one of his heads as if it had been mortally wounded, and his deadly wound was healed. And all the world marveled and followed the beast. 4 So they worshiped the dragon who gave authority to the beast; and they worshiped the beast, saying, "Who is like the beast? Who is able to make war with him?"

5 And he was given a mouth speaking great things and blasphemies, and he was given authority to continue for forty-two months.

If you think satanic worship is rampant today, it will dwarf in comparison to the amount that people would witness near the middle of the Tribulation. Not only would the dragon be worshipped, people will also worship the Antichrist. The Antichrist will morph from a world ruler to a god. Then he would begin to assert his true desire by railing against the true God and His heavenly saints:

REVELATION 13:4-10
So they worshiped the dragon who gave authority to the beast; and they worshiped the beast, saying, "Who is like the beast? Who is able to make war with him?"

5 And he was given a mouth speaking great things and blasphemies, and he was given authority to continue for forty-two months. 6

> *Then he opened his mouth in blasphemy against God, to blaspheme His name, His tabernacle, and those who dwell in heaven. 7 It was granted to him to make war with the saints and to overcome them. And authority was given him over every tribe, tongue, and nation. 8 All who dwell on the earth will worship him, whose names have not been written in the Book of Life of the Lamb slain from the foundation of the world. 9 If anyone has an ear, let him hear. 10 He who leads into captivity shall go into captivity; he who kills with the sword must be killed with the sword. Here is the patience and the faith of the saints.*

The tribulation saints will not cooperate with the Antichrist. When they accept Christ as their Savior, they will be sealed for eternity. They cannot accept the Mark of the Beast after that.

When that time comes, you will only get two choices. You will either accept Christ as your Savior or, you will take the Mark, so that you will be able buy, sell, and trade. The only reason to reject the mark of the beast will be Salvation. That will mean you are refusing to cooperate with the Antichrist. Today, we can accept Christ freely with little adverse consequences to ourselves. Accepting Christ as Savior during the Tribulation will probably have lethal consequences. Either decision will be irreversible. More than likely, accepting Christ will result in martyrdom. Not all Tribulation saints will die. Some will escape the Antichrist's grasp. More on what happens to them during the Millennium later.

So how would the Antichrist get the whole world on his side? He would mimic what Christ went through – death, burial, and resurrection. The Antichrist will match 'this by receiving a fatal wound that should kill him. But power from Satan himself will allow the Antichrist to be healed. When that happens, everyone, including Israel, who will already reject Christ, will think that he is the real deal. They will all be duped into thinking that this guy is the Messiah, bringing in the Kingdom. Satan will also give him power to solve global problems during the first part of the tribulation. Thus, he will go from a military leader to the pinnacle of his desire i.e. to be worshipped as god/ messiah.

So far we've covered the first 42 months or 3 ½ years. The tribulation is divided into 2 equal parts. We're almost half way through it. Let's take a closer look at the last part of the counterfeit trinity:

Event # 12: The False Prophet
Revelation 13: 11-18

Then I saw another beast coming up out of the earth, and he had two horns like a lamb and spoke like a dragon. 12 And he exercises all the authority of the first beast in his presence, and causes the earth and those who dwell in it to worship the first beast, whose deadly wound was healed. 13 He performs great signs, so that he even makes fire come down from heaven on the earth in the sight of men. 14 And he deceives those who dwell on the earth by those signs which he was granted to do in the sight of the beast, telling those who dwell on the earth to make an image to the beast who was wounded by the sword and lived. 15 He was granted power to give breath to the image of the beast, that the image of the beast should both speak and cause as many as would not worship the image of the beast to be killed. 16 He causes all, both small and great, rich and poor, free and slave, to receive a mark on their right hand or on their foreheads, 17 and that no one may buy or sell except one who has the mark or the name of the beast, or the number of his name.

18 Here is wisdom. Let him who has understanding calculate the number of the beast, for it is the number of a man: His number is 666.

In this dispensation of grace, the Holy Spirit draws people to Jesus. No one can be saved without the Spirit moving. Once one accepts Christ, the role of the Holy Spirit continues – He seals, He equips, and He fills the believer (upon request).

The False Prophet, on the other hand, is described as having two horns like a lamb (symbolic of religious character), trying to convince the world of how spiritual he is by the deceptive miracles he performs. He will speak like a dragon; in other words, whatever he communicates will come straight from Satan himself.

Here is the counterfeit Holy Spirit. The Antichrist will do the will of his father or Satan. The False Prophet empowered by Satan will then convince the whole world to worship the seemingly resurrected Antichrist.

He will also convince citizens to make an image of the first beast (Antichrist):

"The image is the center of false worship and the focal point of the final state of apostasy, the acme of the idolatry which has been the false religion of so many generations". [4]

Then the false prophet will apparently give life to the image. More than likely, this will be some sort of holographic image seen in person or broadcasted to all, so they could be duped as the real deal.

This will soon progress towards forced worship. Refusal will of course result in death. Not only will all be forced to worship the Antichrist, they all will also be forced to receive the mark of the beast. The mark will include, but not necessarily be limited to, the number of man 666.

So, Revelation 13 focuses on two beasts empowered by the Dragon (Satan). The first beast is the Antichrist. The second beast is the False Prophet. The first beast will transition from a world ruler to god. The second beast will serve as the catalyst for the transition. The following chart sums up how important the second beast is to the first beast and the Dragon himself:

Ten Identifying Features of the False Prophet

1. He will rise out of the Earth
2. He will control religious affairs
3. He will be motivated by Satan
4. He will promote the worship of the Beast and the Antichrist

[4] Ed Hindson 'Popular Encyclopedia of the Bible' pg. 102

5. He will also perform miracles and signs
6. He will deceive the whole world
7. He will empower the image of the Beast
8. He will also kill all those who refuse to worship
9. He will control the economy of the world
10. He will control the Mark of the Beast

EVENT #13 ONE-WORLD GOVERNMENT, ECONOMY, RELIGION DEVELOPS

I listed this event next but it actually completes events 11, 12. During the first 3 ½ years of the tribulation the Antichrist and his confederation quickly conquer the world.

DANIEL 7:23

Thus he said:
'The fourth beast shall be
A fourth kingdom on earth,
Which shall be different from all other kingdoms,
And shall devour the whole earth,
Trample it and break it in pieces.

We covered The False Prophet's role in assisting the Antichrist to power from Revelation 13. He also assists the Antichrist to take control of a global economy by forcing everyone to take the mark if they want to survive.

Since Pentecost, the Holy Spirit enables and equips believers to have and be the true church of Jesus Christ. During the first half of the Tribulation, the False Prophet counterfeits the Holy Spirit's role except by deception then force.

We currently separate church and state. The church has a right to be involved with matters of the state but the state has no right to be involved with matters of the church. Anytime the two are on equal footing trouble usually ensues. It is no different near the middle of the Tribulation. Just as quickly as the state, economy, and church converge in Babylon (Counterfeit Millennial Jerusalem) to a pinnacle in Revelation 13 it begins to fall apart in events 16, 17, 18. We'll explore this later including chapters 17, 18 of Revelation.

Event # 14: The Antichrist Breaks the Peace Treaty with Israel

'The disciples were wondering about the last days. So Jesus had a lengthy discussion describing when and what the last days would look like. Here is a portion of His 'Olivet Discourse:

Matthew 24:15-22

"Therefore when you see the 'abomination of desolation,' spoken of by Daniel the prophet, standing in the holy place" (whoever reads, let him understand), 16 "then let those who are in Judea flee to the mountains. 17 Let him who is on the housetop not go down to take anything out of his house. 18 And let him who is in the field not go back to get his clothes. 19 But woe to those who are pregnant and to those who are nursing babies in those days! 20 And pray that your flight may not be in winter or on the Sabbath. 21 For then there will be great tribulation, such as has not been since the beginning of the world until this time, no, nor ever shall be. 22 And unless those days were shortened, no flesh would be saved; but for the elect's sake those days will be shortened.

Keep in mind that this information is intended for Israel. This passage describes the beginning of the Great Tribulation. This event divides the 7 years at the very center (3 ½ + 3 ½ = 7). In the first half, Israel enjoys peace, protection, and prosperity under the covenant with the Antichrist and his confederacy. The whole nation will be convinced that the kingdom has begun with the genuine Messiah.

Then this image of the Antichrist will be placed inside the Temple. Doing so, directly violates the Levitical regulations. Daniel 9:27 calls it the abomination that will bring desolation. Its entry into the Temple foreshadows the desecration of the Temple. When that happens, the Levites will no longer serve Jehovah as the Levitical regulations had stipulated.

2 Thessalonians 2:3,4

Let no one deceive you by any means; for that Day will not come unless the falling away comes first, and the man of sin is revealed, the son of perdition, 4 who opposes and exalts himself above all that is called God or that is worshiped, so that he sits as God in the temple of God, showing himself that he is God.

Here, the true nature of the Antichrist will be revealed. He will no longer conceal his intentions to replace Christ as Messiah. Satan will also know his time is running short. Jesus warned Israel to evacuate immediately and travel to any safe place they can find, if they are to avoid genocide.

After the image is placed and the covenant broken, the Antichrist will want to remove all evidence of God and His people. All who refuse the mark of the beast will be sought out for execution. That leads us to:

|15-18 19|

Event # 15: The Saints Are Persecuted

Daniel 7:25

He shall speak pompous words against the most High, and shall persecute the saints of the most High, and shall intend to change times and laws: then the saints shall be given into his hand for a time and times and half a time.

"Likely Satan thinks that if the Jews are exterminated, God's plan for history might be thwarted. Satan might think that this would somehow prevent the second coming."[5]

The Antichrist will kill many of the saints but since he's not Christ he won't be able to kill all saints or all Jews.

Zechariah 13:8,9

It shall come to pass in all the land, says the Lord, two thirds in it shall be cut off and die; one third shall be left.

I will bring the one third part through the fire, and will refine them as silver is refined, and test them as gold is tested: they will call on my name and I will answer them: I will say, It is my people: and each one will say, The Lord is my God.

The third part of the scattered remnant (already tested) will be purified through this great tribulation. Then, when Christ appears

---

[5]Popular Encyclopedia of Bible Prophecy pg. 390

to set up the Millennium, they, along with other believers who escaped, will be called back. They will gladly welcome Christ then become citizens of the kingdom.

Let's be reminded that the tribulation includes the development of a one world government, church, and economy. The counterfeit trinity wants to counterfeit the Millennium. As quickly as everything will develop, it will also fall apart in similar fashion. God is sovereign. He already knows how this will unfold.

Now that the Antichrist has changed everything let's see what he does with the counterfeit church:

Event # 16: Apostate World-Church Gets Destroyed

Revelation 17:1-6

One of the seven angels who had the seven bowls, came and talked with me, saying to me, Come, I will show you the judgment of the great harlot who sits on many waters: With whom the kings of the earth committed fornication, and the inhabitants of the earth were made drunk with the wine of her fornication. So he carried me away in the spirit into the wilderness: and I saw a woman sitting on a scarlet beast, which was full of names of blasphemy, having seven heads and ten horns. The woman was arrayed in purple and scarlet, and adorned with gold and precious stones and pearls, having in her hand a golden cup, full of abominations and filthiness of her fornication: And on her forehead, a name was written, Mystery, Babylon The Great, The Mother Of Harlots And Abominations Of The Earth. I saw the woman drunk with the blood of the saints, and with the blood of the martyrs of Jesus: and when I saw her, I marveled with great admiration.

It is best to interpret Revelation 17 as ecclesiastical Babylon and chapter 18 as economical Babylon. First, let's consider its history.

The Bible is full of information about Babylon as the source of false religion. It all began with the building of the tower of Babel (confusion). Later, it was applied to the city of Babylon 3000 BC under one of the most famous rulers Hammurabi. After a decline, Babylon again rose to the heights under Nebuchadnezzar during Daniel's day. He came 600 years before Christ. His reign and the history of Babylon are the background for the Book of Daniel. Babylon was important both politically and religiously in those days.

Nimrod, who founded the city of Babylon had a wife, Semiramis. Semiramis founded a secret religious rite of Babylon mysteries.

According to accounts outside the Bible, she had a son through a miraculous conception. He was named Tammuz and in effect was a false fulfillment of the promise of the seed of the woman given to Eve.

Various religious practices were observed in connection with this false Babylonian religion. This included recognizing the mother and child as god and creating an order of virgins who became religious prostitutes. Tammuz was killed by a wild animal and was restored to life – a satanic mockery and counterfeit of the resurrection of Christ. Scripture condemns this religion in both Ezekiel and Jeremiah. The worship of Baal is related to the worship of Tammuz.

When Persians took over Babylon in 539 AD, they discouraged the continuation of this religion. Subsequently, cultists moved to Pergamon where one of the seven churches of Asia Minor is located. Chief priests who worshipped the fish god wore crowns in the shape of a fish head. They bore the words, Keeper of the Bridge, symbolic of the bridge between man and Satan.

The Roman Emperors used the Latin title, *pontifus maximus*, meaning major keeper of the bridge later adopted the handle. The same title was given to the Bishop of Rome. Even the Pope is sometimes called the Pontiff. The teachers who practiced the Babylonian religion moved from Pergamon to Rome. Their influence on making Christianity pagan grew. They were the source of many of the so-called religious rites, which has crept into ritualistic Churches.

Babylon then is the symbol of apostasy and blasphemous substitution of idol worship for the worship of God and Christ. In this passage, Revelations 17, Babylon comes to its final judgment[6].

This form of religion comes full circle to where it all began,

---

[6]'Bible Knowledge Commentary' (New Testament pgs. 970,971)

namely the tower of Babel in the city of Babylon built by Nimrod. The tower was built in defiance as a way of saying, we will earn our way to God.

Central to this vision is the rider of the beast. This harlot is actually the one world church headed up by the False Prophet. We touched on him back in Revelation 13. The beast is the kingdom of the antichrist. . The waters are representative of mankind. Now let's look at the destruction.

REVELATION 17:16-18

And the ten horns which you saw on the beast, these will hate the harlot, make her desolate and naked, eat her flesh and burn her with fire. For god has put it in their hearts to fulfill His purpose, to be of one mind, and to give their kingdom to the beast, until the words of god are fulfilled. And the woman whom you saw is that great city which reigns over the kings of the earth.

Since the Antichrist will become the political ruler of the world, he will no longer need the one world church. He will then substitute it for the final stage of apostasy i.e. worship of himself.

Instead of covering the destruction of economical Babylon next, I want to cover three series of judgments from the hand of God that overlay these tribulation events:

Event # 17: Cataclysmic Judgments of God

These judgments will begin near the middle of the tribulation and continue to the end. I believe these judgments are designed to break the world down before God renovates it for the Millennium.

There are 3 sets of 7 judgments. Each set becomes more severe than the previous set. All 21 judgments are listed in Revelation 6-18:

Seal Judgments

Seal # 1

A white horse, a rider with a bow, representing the world government developing without warfare.

Seal # 2

A red horse and a rider, representing taking peace from the Earth. This is the development of the one world government formed by the Antichrist.

Seal # 3

A black horse and a rider holding a set of scales. This is symbolic of a worldwide famine. It will take a day's worth of work just to get three meals.

Seal # 4

A pale horse will represent the loss of one fourth of the world's population due to war, famine, and death.

Seal # 5

Symbolic of the souls under the altar, representing believers who get martyred.

Seal #6

A great earthquake and the sun turns black. The moon turns blood red. Stars fall from the sky like light flares.

Seal # 7

Silence in heaven for half an hour in order to introduce the next set.

Trumpet Judgments

Trumpet Judgment #1

Hail and fire mixed with blood fall upon the Earth. A third of all vegetation destroyed and there is no grass anywhere on Earth,

Trumpet Judgment #2

A burning mountain gets cast into the sea and kills 1/3 rd of all life in every ocean. It destroys a third of all ships on it.

Trumpet Judgment #3

A blazing star, wormwood, gets cast, poisoning 1/3 rd of all freshwater on Earth.

Trumpet Judgment #4

Light is reduced, $1/3^{rd}$ of the sun is now darkened, shortening each day by 8 hours.

Trumpet Judgment #5

Stinging locusts from the abyss come out to torture all those who have taken the mark of the Beast for five months.

Trumpet Judgment #6

Four angels from the Euphrates river come to kill the second third of the world's population. If we use today's numbers 4 out of 6 billion are gone.

Trumpet Judgment #7

Worship in heaven introduces the Bowl Judgments, the most severe set of the three.

Bowl Judgments

Bowl Judgment # 1

Ugly painful sores appear on all who have taken the mark of the beast.

Bowl Judgment # 2

No life in the sea.

Bowl Judgment # 3

No more freshwater because the rest has all turned to blood.

Bowl Judgment # 4

Ozone is depleted.

Bowl Judgment # 5

More darkness and painful sores are visited upon those who took the mark of the Beast.

Bowl Judgment # 6

The Euphrates River dries up and that gives way to the Eastern Army. Two hundred million foot soldiers to come and fight against the Antichrist and all those who have joined them. Three demons come out of the same river bed, convincing everybody to stop fighting each other and focus their attention on Christ coming from heaven.

Bowl Judgment # 7

It is done. Thunder and lightning and earthquakes – worse than all previous earthquakes combined. Resulting in all cities flattened and every island gone.

While the fake millennium would seem to peak in the second half of the tribulation, it would just as quickly begin to fall apart with the global effects of these 21 judgments from the hand of God. Now let's go back to Babylon:

Event # 18: Collapse of the World Commercial System

Revelation 18: 1-24 states that Babylon will become the political, religious, and economical capital of the world, during the second half of the tribulation. Chapter 17 focuses on its religious destruction whereas chapter 18 focuses on the economic downfall of the global commercial system. I believe the seeds of it exist even today. Major events anywhere in the world can trigger market downfall in many countries. Just look at the history of the price of gas. One leaked tanker disaster shoots up the price of gas around the globe.

Babylon's destruction would seem to be in direct proportion to its prominent control of the global economy. Onlookers would react with horror knowing that their lifestyle will disintegrate just as quickly. The city will be up in smoke all within an hour. We can't be specific on the mode of destruction but we can relate it to something like the Sodom & Gomorrah fire bomb from the book of Genesis.

Now that the world will be literally falling apart, those left begin to see an opportunity to assert their dominance on a global scale. The stage would be set for the war of all wars and the battle of all battles:

Event # 19: Armageddon

Some scholars think that a military campaign will reach its peak in the valley of Megiddo. The area is located between the Red and Dead Sea. It is a plain of 1400 sq. miles where all the armies of the world will gather. Their attack would eventually focus on 'Christ's second coming before setting up the true Millennium.

Matthew 24:27-31

27 For as the lightning comes from the east and flashes to the west, so also will the coming of the Son of Man be. 28 For wherever the carcass is, there the eagles will be gathered together.

29 "Immediately after the tribulation of those days the sun will be darkened, and the moon will not give its light; the stars will fall from heaven, and the powers of the heavens will be shaken. 30 Then the sign of the Son of Man will appear in heaven, and then all the tribes of the earth will mourn, and they will see the Son of Man coming on the clouds of heaven with power and great glory. 31 And He will send His angels with a great sound of a trumpet, and they will gather together His elect from the four winds, from one end of heaven to the other.

Let's revisit Bowl judgment #6 which sets the stage for this event.

Revelation 16:12-14, 16

12 Then the sixth angel poured out his bowl on the great river Euphrates, and its water was dried up, so that the way of the kings from the east might be prepared. 13 And I saw three unclean spirits like frogs coming out of the mouth of the dragon, out of the mouth of the beast, and out of the mouth of the false prophet. 14 For they are spirits of demons, performing signs, which go out to the kings of the earth and of the whole world, to gather them to the battle of that great day of God Almighty.

16 And they gathered them together to the place called in Hebrew,

Armageddon.

The destruction of Babylon will then be viewed from a position of weakness by other nations. So, the eastern army will see an opportunity to conquer. Things will become even more intense when all of a sudden the barrier between the two territories dries up, namely the great river Euphrates.

"This reflects a conflict among the nations themselves in the latter portions of the great tribulation as the world empire so hastily put together begins to disintegrate. The armies of the world contending for honors on the battlefield at the very time of the second coming of Christ do all turn, however, and combine their efforts against Christ and His army from heaven when the glory of the second coming appears in the heavens. It will be the final challenge to divine sovereignty and power as the military might of the world of that day will be engaged in fighting on the very day that Christ returns."[7]

This event will be over before Christ's feet will touch the earth.

---

[7] Walvoord, The Revelation of Jesus Christ pg. 237

		20-23 24-25

EVENT # 20: APPEARANCE OF CHRIST ON EARTH

REVELATION 19:11-16

[11] Now I saw heaven opened, and behold, a white horse. And He who sat on him was called Faithful and True, and in righteousness He judges and makes war. [12] His eyes were like a flame of fire, and on His head were many crowns. He had a name written that no one knew except Himself. [13] He was clothed with a robe dipped in blood, and His name is called The Word of God. [14] And the armies in heaven, clothed in fine linen, white and clean, followed Him on white horses. [15] Now out of His mouth goes a sharp sword, that with it He should strike the nations. And He Himself will rule them with a rod of iron. He Himself treads the winepress of the fierceness and wrath of Almighty God. [16] And He has on His robe and on His thigh a name written:

KING OF KINGS AND LORD OF LORDS

Did you notice the armies included in this description? Who will be the soldiers? It will be you and me. After the Judgment seat of Christ (event #4), we get new white clothes, representing righteous acts of the saints. We will also be on white horses. The best part of Armageddon is that all we have to do is show up. Christ will take care of the rest. We only have to get dressed before we come back to Earth, to rule, and reign with Christ for the thousand years.

Revelation 19:17-21

17 Then I saw an angel standing in the sun; and he cried with a loud voice, saying to all the birds that fly in the midst of heaven, "Come and gather together for the supper of the great God, 18 that you may eat the flesh of kings, the flesh of captains, the flesh of mighty men, the flesh of horses and of those who sit on them, and the flesh of all people, free and slave, both small and great." 19 And I saw the beast, the kings of the earth, and their armies, gathered together to make war against Him who sat on the horse and against His army. 20 Then the beast was captured, and with him the false prophet who worked signs in his presence, by which he deceived those who received the mark of the beast and those who worshiped his image. These two were cast alive into the lake of fire burning with brimstone. 21 And the rest were killed with the sword which proceeded from the mouth of Him who sat on the horse. And all the birds were filled with their flesh.

All of the armies gathered there will be devastated when Christ opens his mouth and levels them. The blood will be rise as high as the height of a horse's mouth. Then God will call all the vultures and birds of the sky to come feast on the carnage. All of the armies will be destroyed and all who are left will receive Christ as King, especially Israel.

Event # 21: Binding of Satan In the Bottomless Pit

Revelation 20:1-3

20 Then I saw an angel coming down from heaven, having the key to the bottomless pit and a great chain in his hand. 2 He laid hold of the dragon, that serpent of old, who is the Devil and Satan, and bound him for a thousand years; 3 and he cast him into the bottomless pit, and shut him up, and set a seal on him, so that he should deceive the nations no more till the thousand years were finished. But after these things he must be released for a little while.

The first two recipients of what I call permanent hell or Gehenna will be the antichrist and the false prophet. By that time, Satan would be jailed in a bottomless pit for a thousand years. This Abyss is a place of confinement. The evil trinity will be forever dismantled. Spiritual warfare will not exist.

Since the Garden of Eden, Satan possessed limited power to rule the earth. This power will reach its pinnacle during the tribulation. However, he will have no more influence on earth until the thousand years will be completed.

I believe his release is designed as a test for all the citizens still in their natural bodies. Satan will somehow find hoards of citizens who have head knowledge of Christ but no heart change at his beck and call. More on that with events 24 and 25.

EVENT #22 MILLENNIUM

With the antichrist and False Prophet in Hell and Satan bound in the abyss, God will then renovate the Earth. Nothing but peace and prosperity will exist while Christ rules the world from Jerusalem.

ISAIAH 9:7

7 Of the increase of His government and peace
There will be no end,
Upon the throne of David and over His kingdom,
To order it and establish it with judgment and justice
From that time forward, even forever.
The zeal of the Lord of hosts will perform this.

All will be similar to how it used to be with Adam and Eve before the fall. The curse of sin on earth will be removed. Adam and Eve knew not hard labor before the sin's curse. All they had to do was take care of the Garden of Eden. During the Millennium, the world will revert to that form. The curse of sin on the earth will be reversed.

ISAIAH 30:23-24

23 Then He will give the rain for your seed
With which you sow the ground,
And bread of the increase of the earth;
It will be fat and plentiful.
In that day your cattle will feed
In large pastures.
24 Likewise the oxen and the young donkeys that work the ground
Will eat cured fodder,
Which has been winnowed with the shovel and fan.

The animal kingdom will be changed for the better.

Isaiah 65:25

25 The wolf and the lamb shall feed together,
The lion shall eat straw like the ox,
And dust shall be the serpent's food.
They shall not hurt nor destroy in all My holy mountain,"
Says the Lord.

Satan, the prince and power of the air, won't run the world anymore. Christ will rule and reign from Jerusalem while all other citizens would participate under a perfect government and economy.

Those who did not get killed during the tribulation will live in their natural bodies (still capable of sinning) and begin to repopulate the Earth. The average lifespan will extend to the end of the 1000 years. Death will still occur but there will be little need for hospitals. Before the Flood, people used to live an average of 500 years or more. Those numbers will appear again during the Millennium.

But Sinners who give birth to more sinners will be citizens of the Kingdom but not necessarily children of the king. At the end of those thousand years, they will play a role of rebellion when Satan is released from the pit.

"So, the millennium will be a time in which the edenic curse of sin will be rolled back. The earth will be renovated to edenic conditions. Christ will rule the world from the throne of David. He will bring peace and righteousness. It will be a time of great spiritual triumph in which national Israel will fulfill her destiny. The gentiles will partake of tremendous blessings through Christ and the nation of Israel. The bible describes the millennium as a time of righteousness, obedience, holiness, truth, and fullness of spirit, as never before. It will be a time of environmental transformation. Isaiah talks about it in the 35th chapter, saying that the desert will blossom and become productive. There will be an abundance of rainfall in areas that today are known for their dryness. There will be plenty of food for animals. In addition, the predatory instincts of the animals will cease. The distinction between tame and wild will be erased. All creatures will coexist."[8]

Average life spans will be lengthened tremendously partly because of the reversed curse on the earth.

Isaiah 65:20
20 "No more shall an infant from there live but a few days,
Nor an old man who has not fulfilled his days;
For the child shall die one hundred years old,
But the sinner being one hundred years old shall be accursed.

100 years will still be considered the age of a child. That number reflects pre flood days when the average lifespan was well over 500 years.

The spiritual characteristics of the kingdom will focus on worship at the newly constructed temple, described in Ezekiel chapters 40-46. The measurements of this temple far exceed previous versions. It seems to me that offerings in the previous temples will continue here but only to serve as memorials.

Nothing will hinder worship. Pilgrimage to Jerusalem will be the norm, not the exception. Sinning saints, as well as glorified saints will regularly travel long distances to get to church.

"So to sum up this divine global kingdom, we will experience the following characteristics:

- Joy
- Glory

---

[8] Charting the End Times, Tim Lahaye pg. 70

- Justice
- Full Knowledge
- Instruction & Learning
- Removal of Curse on Earth
- Longevity of Life
- Prosperity in Work
- Harmony in Animal Kingdom" [9]

Soon we will be able to experience life on earth as it was originally intended to be experienced. The spiritual kingdom that Christ offered on a Palm Sunday is on its way today. Even though we in America enjoy freedom of worship without government interference, we will one day enjoy the perfect union of church and state.

I look forward to the true one world government, economy, and church. Beware of the counterfeit!

---

[9] Joe Jordan, The Popular Encyclopedia Of Bible Prophecy pg. 236

Event # 23: Resurrection of Tribulation Saints

Revelation 20:4-6

4 And I saw thrones, and they sat on them, and judgment was committed to them. Then I saw the souls of those who had been beheaded for their witness to Jesus and for the word of God, who had not worshiped the beast or his image, and had not received his mark on their foreheads or on their hands. And they lived and reigned with Christ for a thousand years. 5 But the rest of the dead did not live again until the thousand years were finished. This is the first resurrection. 6 Blessed and holy is he who has part in the first resurrection. Over such the second death has no power, but they shall be priests of God and of Christ, and shall reign with Him a thousand years.

Why are the tribulation-saints being resurrected here? It is a part of God's plan. These martyrs lost their lives during the tribulation. They had accepted Christ as their Savior, which came at a hefty price. The Antichrist caught them and killed them for refusing to take the mark of the beast. The souls of martyred tribulation saints will be reunited with their resurrected bodies near the beginning of the millennium and then be rewarded with positions of leadership in the kingdom.

Event # 24: Satan Freed From The Bottomless Pit

Revelation 20:7

7 Now when the thousand years have expired, Satan will be released from his prison

This has baffled me for years. Why would God give him an opportunity to oppose Christ and the kingdom? The only possibility that makes sense to me is to test the hearts of citizens. In dispensational theology, it is said that God tests humankind in accordance to a particular time they live in. The test in verse 7 will bring to the surface those who only comply with Christ and his kingdom. I believe God will use Satan to reveal the hearts of those who are unsaved and force them to make a choice similar to test of people during the tribulation.

Event # 25: Satan Leads Unsaved Men Against God

Revelation 20:8-9

8 and will go out to deceive the nations which are in the four corners of the earth, Gog and Magog, to gather them together to battle, whose number is as the sand of the sea. 9 They went up on the breadth of the earth and surrounded the camp of the saints and the beloved city. And fire came down from God out of heaven and devoured them.

Due to the immense population growth from the natural survivors of the tribulation, John has described them as uncountable. They will be easy marks due to not having many temptations in such a comfortable lifestyle. Since Satan knows our weaknesses, he will be quick to spot theirs and tempt them in similar fashion. He tempted Adam and Eve in the same way by convincing them that God was holding out on them lest they become like Him (which is Satan's supreme desire in Isaiah 14:12-14.)

Govett suggests 4 reasons Satan is allowed this opportunity:[10]

1. To demonstrate that man will fall into sin if left to his own choice, even under the most favorable circumstances.
2. To demonstrate the foreknowledge of God who foretells the acts of men, as well as, His own acts.
3. To demonstrate the incurable wickedness of Satan
4. To justify eternal punishment

---

[10] Robert Govett, The Apocalypse Expounded, pgs. 506-08

Event # 26: Satan Defeated

Revelation 20:9
9and fire came down from God out of heaven, and devoured them.

God has used fire from heaven as a form of judgment on different occasions. Christ will exact a similar judgment at His second coming where he will open his mouth and breathe out fire. The fire will destroy everything in the valley of Megiddo.

Walvoord comments, "Thus is shattered the last vain attempt of Satan to claim a place of prominence and worship in attempted usurpation of the prerogatives of God. Thus ends also the false theory that man under perfect environment will willingly serve the God who created and redeemed him. This is the end of the road for the nations who rebel against God as well as for the career of Satan." [11]

Ever since the Garden of Eden, Satan has been out to rob, kill, and destroy. Here he meets his end. No longer will he be able to tempt, influence, or possess anyone. All that's left for him is to suffer without relief. He will enter his eternal dwelling that was originally created for him and all who followed him from heaven.

Isaiah 14:12
"How you are fallen from heaven,
O Lucifer, son of the morning!

---

[11] Walvoord, The Revelation Of Jesus Christ, pg. 304

How you are cut down to the ground,
You who weakened the nations!
I look forward to be able to tell him where to go.

Event # 27: Satan Cast Into The Lake Of Fire

Revelation 20:10

10 The devil, who deceived them, was cast into the lake of fire and brimstone where the beast and the false prophet are. And they will be tormented day and night forever and ever.

Even though both are hell, Gehenna (Lake of Fire) is permanent compared to Hades. If you become a participant in Hades, then you are already in hell. Eventually, everyone in Hades will get a short reprieve only to be judged and then cast into permanent hell or Gehenna. The antichrist and the false prophet, according to event 19, will already be in permanent hell. Satan will join them at the end of the millennium.

God created hell for the evil angels who left with Satan. It wasn't intended for humans. However, the unsaved will be sent there because they rejected God's provision for sin. Humans who reject the knowledge from God available to them, regardless of the age they live in, will be sent to permanent hell. In this event, Satan becomes the third recipient of the Lake Of Fire.

Event # 28: Great White Throne of Judgment & Resurrection of Unsaved Dead

This is different from the judgment seat of Christ. The Beama will reveal works of ministry. The GWT will reveal every sin, especially the rejection of Christ.

Revelation 20:11
11 Then I saw a great white throne and Him who sat on it, from whose face the earth and the heaven fled away. And there was found no place for them.

Revelation 20:12
12 And I saw the dead, small and great, standing before God, and books were opened. And another book was opened, which is the Book of Life. And the dead were judged according to their works, by the things which were written in the books.

God has perfectly recorded every deed of everyone who will stand at this judgment. In the previous judgment, sin was not recorded because Christ took care of that. In this judgment, every sin by every individual who has rejected God will be brought up. Since the passage says books were opened, there was more than one book. Included in the group was the book of life.

The book of life records the life of every individual i.e. not the eternal life but that they were born. The lamb's book life is another book that is different from the book of life. It is mentioned in the verse below:

Revelation 21: 27
But there shall by no means enter it anything that defiles, or causes an abomination or a lie, but only those who are written in the Lamb's Book of Life.

So, this book contains the names of everyone who has ever put their trust in God, regardless of when that happened. All the people who trusted in the revelation given to them during their lifetime have their names in this book, going from Adam and Eve, to present day. We know that if our name is not written in this book of life, then we are doomed for the Lake of Fire.

Everyone who will be resurrected from the dead (separated from God since their last breath) is unsaved. They will appear for this judgment.

Paul best sums it up in:

Philippians 2:10-11
[10] that at the name of Jesus every knee should bow, of those in heaven, and of those on earth, and of those under the earth, [11] and that every tongue should confess that Jesus Christ is Lord, to the glory of God the Father.

Wouldn't it be much better to bow the knee and confess now while there's still time and hope? If one waits until this event, it will be too late. But make no mistake, the knee will bend, and the tongue will speak the words JESUS IS LORD.

Event # 29: Judgment of Sin & Punishment of Lake of Fire

Revelation 20:13-15

¹³ The sea gave up the dead who were in it, and Death and Hades delivered up the dead who were in them. And they were judged, each one according to his works. ¹⁴ Then Death and Hades were cast into the lake of fire. This is the second death. ¹⁵ And anyone not found written in the Book of Life was cast into the lake of fire.

I believe the worst part of the Lake of Fire is the separation from God forever. God has placed inside every person the capacity to know Him. It is a spot that only He can fill. The emptiness that will be experienced for eternity will keep that spot empty in a never ending way.

The first death happens when one takes their last breath. This is when the body and soul separate. The soul will go to either heaven or hell for eternity while the body is left behind, regardless of how it will be buried. The unsaved dead soul will appear before Christ and then be permanently separated from God.

This is the second death.

Luke 16: 26

²⁶ And besides all this, between us and you there is a great gulf fixed, so that those who want to pass from here to you cannot, nor can those from there pass to us.'

Hell (Hades & Gehenna) is real. Hell is total separation from God. Hell is loneliness. Hell is total darkness. Hell is total torture. Hell never ends.

As totally undesirable as Hell is, Heaven is the extreme opposite.

Event # 30: New Heaven, Earth, and Jerusalem

Isaiah 65:17

17 For behold, I create new heavens and a new earth; And the former shall not be remembered or come to mind.

The new earth is going to be so spectacular that no one will be longing for the old one. There are three heavens; the first one is sky, the second is the atmosphere, and the third is the Throne of God. God is going to destroy the heavens. He is also going to destroy the earth that was enjoyed during the Millennium and create it anew.

Revelation 21:1-2

21 Now I saw a new heaven and a new earth, for the first heaven and the first earth had passed away. Also there was no more sea. 2 Then I, John, saw the holy city, New Jerusalem, coming down out of heaven from God, prepared as a bride adorned for her husband.

It is going to be a tremendous city upon which Christ is finishing up now. To demonstrate how big the city is going to be, let us take a road trip. It is going to be as wide as the distance from Coastal North Carolina to Dallas. Not only is it going to be wide, it is also going to be 1400 miles long. It is also going to be 1400 miles high. It is being prepared by Christ in heaven and is just about finished. The city, New Jerusalem, will come down from the heavens. Whether it would remain suspended above the New Earth or rest on it, I am not sure. Either way it will be home for all who have placed their trust in God during their lifetime.

The rest of chapter 21 describes brilliant aspects of this 1,400 mile cubed city. It will have 12 foundations of stones. Each foundation is one stone. No measurement is given of the thickness. But the length and width support the entire city twelve foundations deep.

In addition to the foundations, there will be 12 gates. Three gates facing each direction. Each gate will be a single pearl.

During the Millennium, a temple larger than any temple that has ever been made will be built. However, in New Jerusalem, there will be no need for a temple. God permeates the entire eternal state. In addition to its size and beauty, John sees more uniqueness in that city:

Revelation 22:1-2

22 And he showed me a pure river of water of life, clear as crystal, proceeding from the throne of God and of the Lamb. ² In the middle of its street, and on either side of the river, was the tree of life, which bore twelve fruits, each tree yielding its fruit every month. The leaves of the tree were for the healing of the nations.

Do you find healing odd? Why would there be a need to heal when in an age of perfection? The word heal is actually used in the sense of therapy. The leaves of this tree will have therapeutic properties. The last mention of this tree was when it in the Garden of Eden. Once the death sentence was issued, an angel was stationed there to keep Adam and Eve from going back to the garden to eat the fruit again to thus living in their sinful state forever.

We do not know when it was removed from the Garden of Eden but we know that God will plant it on the new earth, so that everybody can enjoy it and be therapeutically reminded of God's provision.

God will annihilate heaven earth and Jerusalem, then recreate them for eternity. It is hard to imagine a time when there will be no need of time anymore. Time will become irrelevant in eternity. We will be with God, just as Jesus is now. This is why; I have named this study, from the Rapture to Eternity.

Conclusion

Amazing things are about to happen. I believe we are close to the Rapture because we have the super-sign from God today. It happened in 1948 when Israel became a nation again. They are our super-sign. I tell people to keep their ears open and their eyes on the temple mount. Doing so will help us be ready for His return in the sky.

No one can separate true believers from God once they have accepted Christ as their Savior. No one can lose their salvation because they didn't earn it. Christ earned it for them. However, those who haven't are in for a rude awakening.

If you have never accepted Christ as Savior, there is no better time than now. The good news is simple: Admit your sin. Agree that Christ died for your sin. Ask Jesus to Save you. Do this while you have breath. Eternity is too long to be wrong.

God has given us everything we need to know about the future in His word. This book is heavy on Scripture by design. It's not about what I think. It's about what God says. His word is eternal. His word is reliable. His word is all we need for faith and Christian living.

This book barely touches the surface of Eschatology (doctrine of last things). My goal was to present in outline form thirty major prophetic events yet to take place. I hope I presented it in a way that is easily understandable. I hope you get the big picture. But most of all I hope you get Jesus:

Revelation 22:12-13

12 And, behold, I come quickly; and my reward is with me, to give every man according as his work shall be. 13 I am Alpha and Omega, the beginning and the end, the first and the last.

Made in the USA
Columbia, SC
24 November 2024